There's a Little
Magick
in Every Girl

There's a Little Magick in Every Girl

MIDIA STAR

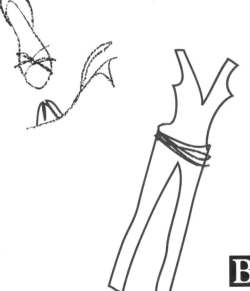

BARRON'S

FIRST EDITION FOR THE UNITED STATES AND
CANADA, AND THE PHILIPPINE REPUBLIC PUBLISHED
IN 2005 BY BARRON'S EDUCATIONAL SERIES, INC.

FIRST PUBLISHED IN GREAT BRITAIN IN 2005 BY
GODSFIELD PRESS, A DIVISION OF OCTOPUS
PUBLISHING GROUP LIMITED, 2–4 HERON QUAYS,
LONDON E14 4JP, GREAT BRITAIN

All inquiries should be addressed to:
BARRON'S EDUCATIONAL SERIES, INC.
250 WIRELESS BOULEVARD
HAUPPAUGE, NEW YORK 11788
http://www.barronseduc.com

International Standard Book Number
0-7641-5846-5
Library of Congress Catalog Card No.
2004096278

Printed in China
9 8 7 6 5 4 3 2 1

Contents

Introduction

It's tough being the fairer sex, isn't it? It's not enough that we have to be as good, if not better, than our male counterparts to get along in this world, we've got to look gorgeous at the same time! You've obviously been drawn to this book for a reason. Whatever that reason is, you can be assured that I have no intention of preaching to you or telling you how you should be living your life. As with the art of witchcraft and Wicca, this book is all about choice. It is designed to show you how it can help you with issues such as making magickal relationships, looking gorgeous, passing exams or tests, banishing bullies, coping with peer pressure and even how to finance that passion for designer handbags – and all in a magickal way.

Although Wicca is commonly seen as a religion, it is not about praying, preaching, or confessing your sins to someone you hardly know. There is only one hard-and-fast rule in Wicca – *you can do whatever you like, so long as you don't hurt anyone in the process* – and this includes feelings and emotions. Other than that it's a free world.

So, you're wondering, who am I to tell you all this then?

Well for a start, I'm a girl – well, a young woman now, but still a girlie girl at heart. I've followed the path of witchcraft since the age of 12, when I discovered this thing called Wicca that seemed to answer all my questions in a sensible and nonjudgmental way. I trained as a journalist, which means I take nothing at face value and research everything to death! I've researched and studied the subject of witchcraft for many years, and I certainly wouldn't have wasted my

time in doing so if I thought it was a bunch of baloney. And as it was not that long ago that, like you, I was a girl demanding answers and protesting, "*Why* can't I do that?" I can still remember how it felt to be in a world where no one seemed to want to explain the answers to my questions.

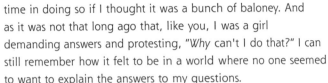

So whether it is a worry, a problem, a situation, or just somewhere to give you the answers to questions such as "What's it all about?" I hope that this book sheds some light on the things that concern you right now.

And this book is dedicated to you – to every girl who wants to know what magick is all about and how she can use it to answer all those confusing questions and live a magickal life!

What is witchcraft?

Okay, first and foremost witchcraft has nothing whatsoever to do with the devil — this little guy is a Christian belief and if you're not a Christian, as witches aren't, then the devil means nothing to you. Neither does it have anything to do with summoning evil spirits, cursing someone, riding a broomstick, or having a cackle.

Witchcraft is the practical side of the Wiccan religion. The religion was first introduced by pagans long before Christianity came along and was in fact a way of life for people rather than a religion as such. People would worship, pray, and give thanks, to not just one god, but to the gods and goddesses of the entire universe, and they respect the views of other people's religions. So pay no attention to anyone who tells you that you are anti-Christian because you don't worship the Christian God.

The only reason witches, as with any minority group, have been given a bad name is mainly due to being misunderstood — in the same way as if you dress differently than your friends do, or live an alternative lifestyle. If people don't share the same ideas as you do they think you're a bit odd. Witchcraft is about embracing life and trying to make the world a better place for everyone, regardless of faith, religion, color, creed, or sex.

Wicca is a very nature-based belief and we use the seasons, herbs, colors, candles, the moon, and the sun to help with spells to attain our dreams and desires, and the dreams and desires of others. Just as in years gone by when people would cast a spell to help a crop grow, today we cast similar spells to help us get along in this modern world. It could be to help you get that first job you want, to have a happy relationship with your boyfriend, or to help out with your finances when you're broke.

As I said, witches are just like any other person on the planet, except they are passionate about what they do and generally get what they want out of life. They aren't sheep following the flock, and they believe that everyone should have the choice to do whatever they like and follow whatever religion they choose, if they so wish. We have freedom of thought and a close union and respect with nature. This is one of the reasons why many girls like you turn to witchcraft, because it has no hard-and-fast rules and regulations that *must* be followed.

It works on the basis that *you* have the power to choose everything you do with your life. If you do something that you know to be morally wrong, then you will have to accept the consequences of your actions. We respect and worship many gods and goddesses who we believe control the entire universe – we will talk about these later in the book – and in turn, these deities help us in our quest for a happy and fulfilling life. And by worship, I don't mean dropping to your knees and praying. The Goddess is all around us all the time. A mere word of thanks, or even just a "good morning," makes the Goddess happy and, in return, much like a genie in a lamp, she grants us what we need and desire.

Witchy myths

Because of movies, books, and the media, witches have always been portrayed as something they are not. Harry Potter, Sabrina the Teenage Witch, *and* Buffy the Vampire Slayer *are all fantastic viewing, but not what witchcraft is all about. Witches can't fly, become invisible, zap people into oblivion, jump into and out of spell books, or recite a few words and make time stand still.*

In movies, witches have a host of "magickal" tools of the trade, but these are not requirements to perform magick. It doesn't cost anything to be a witch. You don't have to wear a black dress and a pointy hat, and invest your hard-earned cash in a supply of broomsticks. After all, there weren't any New Age shops around to pop into when the Druids and pagans practiced The Craft and they managed well enough. So remember, don't believe everything you read, hear, or see about witches. Most of it is make-believe to enhance viewing figures!

Witchcraft was and still is about using the power of nature to help you in whatever situation needs fixing. It's not about buying an assortment of items: these are just magick commercialism. The only things you really need are a book to guide you and natural ingredients that are all easy to buy from a supermarket or readily available from nature. So save your money and don't buy into the hype.

Just like other people, witches come in all shapes and sizes and look no different from you. Okay, so you do get the odd handful of eccentrics who want to shout their belief from the rooftops and declare this by

dressing in an unusual style – decked out from head to toe in black and wearing an assortment of magick symbols. However, the majority of witches dress just like you. I'm just a normal mom to three young daughters, and prior to a career in journalism and writing I worked in a number of jobs, including as a secretary, a vet's assistant, and in a shoe shop. My usual attire is jeans and a T-shirt and the only time I wear a black cloak and a pointy hat is if I'm going to a costume party.

So, as you can see, witches are just like any other person, they simply have the special gift of having someone to call upon when the going gets tough. And it doesn't get more tough than being a girl, does it?

Celebrations

It is interesting to note that many of the Christian celebrations derive from pagan, Druid, and Celtic celebrations. Yes, that's right, witches didn't copy the Christian beliefs and traditions, it was the other way around. Early Christians were unsure of the accurate date for the birth of Christ. Although there were a number of different religions, many people were pagan prior to Christianity, so they decided to use many of the pagan traditions for their own celebrations of Christ. Witches follow and celebrate the cycles of the seasons with special days known as sabbats. For example, instead of celebrating Christmas, we celebrate Yule, which is on December 21. Yule represents the rebirth of the pagan gods and goddesses. The pine tree that is traditionally decorated by Christians celebrating Christmas is also used at Yule and is known as the wish tree, when all your wishes for the new year will come true. The traditional wreath that we see hung on doors at Christmas represents the wheel of the year to witches.

Dark magick

This book is designed to show you how white witchcraft can help you to have a happy and wonderful life and make all your dreams become a reality. It is something that should be taken seriously and not messed with. You've probably come across, or heard about, the darker side of witchcraft.

However tempting it is to dabble in the dark side of witchcraft, please don't. You never know what you may conjure up. The same goes for voodoo. Don't think that by sticking a load of pins into an effigy of someone who has hurt you, you'll get revenge. You won't. Zapping your zits with magick or sorting out your love life is harmless enough, but playing with the dark side of magick destroys people, so please don't even contemplate it.

I knew of one young man who thought it was a good idea to play around with the Ouija board. He asked it many questions, but laughed it off when the Ouija board told him that he would die before he was 21. He killed himself on his 21st birthday. Whether this statement was embedded in his subconscious, we will never know. All I do know is that playing with the dark side of magick may be seen as rebellious now, but you have to bear the long-term consequences.

Ouija boards, voodoo dolls, devil worshipping, and cursing play no role in witchcraft. Neither do sacrificing children, eating toads, growing warts, or conjuring up evil spirits. If this is the road you wish to take, then this book isn't for you. If, however, you wish to have a life full of everything a girl could dream of, then this book is the ideal tool.

A few simple rules

"I thought witchcraft was about free living, no rules, and so on ..."
I hear you say. Yes it is, but as with everything in life, without
some guidelines the world would fall apart. So I'm afraid you do
have to adhere to a few guidelines when you invite witchcraft into
your life. This is because without listening to and learning the
rules of witchcraft, you will be ill-equipped to perform magick,
which will result in spells not working, going wrong, or even
hurting yourself or someone else in the process.

The Threefold Law

Whatever you do in life, be it good or bad, will come back to you three times.

In fact, it can often come back to you up to seven times. Put simply this means that if you do something that you know in your heart is not right, at some point in your life you will be paid back for it.

The Wiccan Reed

Yes, another rule, but a very important one. The Wiccan Reed is one that all witches live by and is that: *You can do whatever you like in your life, so long as you don't hurt anyone or anything.*

Again, think about the consequences of your actions prior to carrying them out. If you're going to be a true witch and true to yourself, think about other people's feelings before you fly off the handle and do or say something that will hurt them, however much they deserve it. Remember the Threefold Law, whoever hurts you will be paid back three times, so don't try to take matters into your own hands.

13

How magick can help you

Practical magick helps you to attain goals and make dreams become a reality. The wonderful thing about magick, or The Craft as it's also known, is that you don't necessarily have to devote your entire life to it. The magickal skills you learn will always be there for you to call upon when you're down, need to find peace, or if you have a problem that needs solving.

You may be wondering why we don't spell magick the usual way (magic): this is simply to show that The Craft has nothing to do with card tricks or pulling a rabbit out of a hat. Magick works hand in hand with your belief system. If you believe strongly enough that you can do something then there is nothing and no one that can stop you from achieving it.

Understanding magick

Practical witchcraft can help anyone and everyone, regardless of age, but because this book is written with you in mind, I have purposely focused on how it can help you in the situations that you probably face on a daily basis: you might have boyfriend troubles, you might not be able to get a boyfriend, you might have parent problems, a problem with liking yourself, self-harm, sexuality, drugs, peer pressure, pregnancy, moral questions, family, appearance, exams, your first job.

One of the most important things you can remember throughout life, though, is that things pass. Whatever mess you might encounter, whatever trouble you may experience in life, however much sadness or confusion you may feel, eventually it always passes. It's how life is meant to be. So, however intolerable a situation may be, believe me, it isn't going to last forever. It will pass and you will move on.

Although I advise you in this book how to perform a spell successfully, you don't *have* to perform a ritual in any specific way. You don't *have* to set up an altar if you don't want, or you can't. Some witchcraft books and information out there can be very misleading to witch-wannabes! They will tell you a list of *must have's* and *must do's*. These "musts" are not necessary: many are just props. I can guarantee you that a spell will work even if you don't have the right colored candle or do a spell when the moon isn't quite right. The moon phases, candles, herbs, and all the other requirements listed in any spell, will

help a spell to work quicker, but are not "musts." For any spell all you need is the belief that it will work and to have faith in yourself and belief in yourself and your powers.

What witchcraft won't do

Witchcraft will not make someone do something they wouldn't normally do. So, for example, doing a love spell to get the guy down the road to ask you out will not work if he is not remotely interested in you in the first place. A love spell can only suggest. It won't force someone to do something they wouldn't usually do and to try will only result in disaster for you and the other person involved.

17

How and why does magick work?

Good question! Without going into too much detail, it's a combination of things. Most of us use only a tiny percentage of the power within us. The magick in this book is known as sympathetic magick, which means using physical objects to get magickal results. When we learn how to tap into our belief system and combine it with the practicalities of magick, we create magick in our lives. The universe is a magickal place, full of possibilities. When we believe in ourselves and call upon the power of nature and the universe to help us, our wishes come true for everything we want in our life — and yes, that includes material things such as that fab dress you want!

Don't shout about it!

Okay, so once you've discovered that witchcraft actually works, you're happy and content in the knowledge that for any problem or situation you may face in life, you can simply cast a spell and make it all better. You can have anything you want and you have the power to make your dreams come true. So you're going to tell all your friends, family, in fact, everyone you know, right? *Wrong!*

I know it's tempting to tell someone that the reason you got the latest cell phone was because you cast a spell, but you are looking for trouble if you shout from the rooftops that you're a witch and can work magick.

Not everyone is open to new ways of thinking and, sad as it may seem, there are still people out there who will discriminate against you for being different from the norm.

Keep it to yourself. Your friends will soon see how great every area of your life is and will naturally begin to wonder why their lives aren't the same. If they are genuinely interested and ask how come you're so upbeat and why everything seems to be going well for you, you can tell them that you practice magick. You could even show them this book; but don't go around telling everyone you come across.

Witchcraft works in mysterious ways

Witchcraft doesn't always work in the way that we might imagine. From years of experience of working with magick, I can guarantee you that spell casting does work, but the results may come in a different way than you think they will. Here's an example: Sam has just started her first job as an illustrator and is being bullied by another member of the staff. She has tried everything she can think of to stop it, including confronting the bully and telling her boss, but to no avail. Sam eventually decides to perform a spell to banish the bully. Weeks pass and nothing happens. Sam is miserable every minute that she's at work because of this bully. Suddenly the girl who is responsible for Sam's misery is fired for stealing supplies from the stockroom. Sam can now get on with her life and enjoy her new job without fearing this one person who has been making her so unhappy.

The moon's helping hand

The moon emits no actual light itself. The bright light that we see from the moon is in fact the reflected light from the sun. However, the moon has always played a big part in our lives down here on Earth. You will have noticed that, throughout the month, the moon changes shape. These changes are known as phases. There are four main phases that the moon travels through every 28 days, which is how long the moon takes to revolve around the Earth. The phases are — the full moon, the waning moon, the waxing moon, and the new moon, or dark moon as it is sometimes called.

Over the years astronomers and astrologers have discovered that the moon has a great influence on our lives. Studies have shown that crime increases during the full moon and that people who are mentally unstable become more agitated during a full moon — so the stories you've heard about werewolves and Dr. Jekyll and Mr. Hyde are not so far from the truth! I once had a boyfriend who became moody and irritable whenever there was a full moon in the sky — I don't think he was a werewolf, but I didn't stick around long enough to find out!

The moon also affects the spells and magick we do. Although it is not necessary to perform a spell in a particular moon phase, it will help the magick to work quicker for you.

• For spells for attracting things to you, such as a new car or new clothes, you should cast a spell on a full moon.

• For spells for banishing things, such as a bully, zapping those zits, and so on, you should cast a spell on a new (dark) moon and when you can't see the moon in the sky.

• If you want to decrease something, such as a credit card debt or a friend who's become a pain in the butt, you should cast a spell on a waning moon (when the moon looks like a C-shape in the sky).

• If you want to increase something in your life, such as money or new friends, then you should cast a spell on a waxing moon (when the moon looks like a D-shape in the sky).

Don't panic if this is a little confusing. In every spell in this book I will tell you which phase of the moon is best to cast that specific spell.

Other useful tools

If you're anything like me you absolutely adore candles, particularly the scented ones. Well, candles can play an important part in spell casting. The flame from a candle can be one of the most powerful vehicles to carry a wish into the universe and this is why most witches use candles in their spells. It doesn't matter if you can get only white candles because white is universal and will work happily with any spell. Different colored candles for different spells are as follows:

- Red/pink – use for encouraging love, peace, harmony, and everything mushy and gushy.
- Black/blue – use for banishing things you don't want in your life, such as ex-boyfriends.
- Green – use for attracting money to pay that huge phone bill you've run up!
- Gold/orange – use these colors to enrich your life or career.

Again, all the spells in this book will tell you what to use and when, but always be careful when using candles. Put your candle in a candle holder, use safety matches or a lighter, and blow out the candle if you are leaving the room for any length of time.

Gods and goddesses

Remember I spoke earlier about there not being just one god, but several in the eyes of the Wiccan religion. Although we say that we ask for help from the Goddess, it is widely believed that different gods and goddesses help us with different things in life. So, for example, if you were casting a spell to find love, you would ask Aphrodite, the goddess of love to help you. If you were thinking of forming a band, you would call upon Apollo, the son of Zeus and god of musicians. All the gods and goddesses come from ancient times, many being Greek. Here are a few that we ask to help us in witchcraft:

• Hera – The wife of the god Zeus, and is associated with women, marriage, and childbirth.
• Hestia – A goddess of protection who grants wishes for the home.
• The Muses – The nine daughters of Zeus and Hera. They are true girlie girls – would you believe pictures show them dancing around their handbags! These girls will help you with any problem you have as a girl.
• Isis – Known by different names but Isis is primarily known as the goddess of womankind. She is the goddess most female witches call upon for help.

The magick cauldron

Okay, so now that you know the basics of working with witchcraft, we can get on with the fun stuff – the spells! This chapter is dedicated to solving every problem imaginable. Whether it's a problem getting a date, you feel your parents just don't understand you, you have problems making or keeping friends, or you just need a little extra cash in your bank account, every girlie situation will have a solution here.

Please remember, though, that witchcraft isn't the easy way out. If you perform a spell without feeling or belief, or think that every time you have a problem you can simply turn to witchcraft, it won't work. The Goddess is there for you at any time, but she doesn't like to be misused. If you start casting spells for the sheer fun of it, she will trip you up by sending you a sign of some kind. Spells work best when you have a real need for something in your life, so only cast a spell when you need to.

Occasionally you might find that a spell doesn't work. If this happens, don't despair. There is a reason why spells don't work sometimes. You might have just come out of a bad relationship and feel desperate to find another boyfriend. However, if you're still hurting inside, the Goddess might think you need some time to yourself to really get over the guy who broke your heart. You might not be ready to fall head over heels again just yet. You might have cast a spell to achieve your dream job, and failed to get past the first interview stage. What if it turned out to be a really horrible place to work? Or, it isn't really your ideal job, it's what your parents want for you and you would really prefer to travel around the world for a year.

If you cast a spell and it really is what you desire, but it doesn't work, check that you're casting it in the right moon phase, or change the spell slightly. For example: say you want to do a spell to increase your finances, but the moon is in the waning (banishing) phase. Change the words in your spell from attracting money, to banishing money worries. If this doesn't work, wait 28 days and re-cast the spell. If you still have no success, then consider if your desire really is what is good for you.

Walking into love spell

There's someone out there for everyone, so never worry if you haven't kissed a boy, let alone had a boyfriend yet. As I mentioned earlier, witchcraft cannot force someone in particular to date you, but if you are tired of being boyfriendless, try this spell to attract the right guy for you into your life. Remember, relationships should be fun, so don't go getting all heavy and cast a spell to find your one and only true love for life!

Ingredients

- Some rose oil
- A pink candle
- A candle holder
- Matches or a lighter
- A piece of pink paper
- Scissors
- A pinch of rose talcum powder

Cast this spell on a full moon if you can, or on a Friday night. Friday is the day dedicated to the goddess of love and this is the ideal time to cast any spells to do with matters of the heart.

Put three drops of rose oil in your hand and wipe the oil all over the pink candle. Place the candle in a candle holder and light it. Say the following words three times:

By the power of light
Upon this night
I send a message of love
To the universe above
So as I walk
Let me bump into the guy who is right for me
This is my wish, so mote it be.

Cut two small hearts out of a piece of pink paper and put a few drops of rose oil on them. Place the hearts in a pair of shoes or trainers that you wear often and sprinkle a small amount of rose talcum powder into each shoe. Wear your "magick shoes" when you go out again. You never know who you might bump into!

Call me spell

It is so annoying when you find yourself sitting by the phone just waiting for him to call, isn't it? Should you call him? Maybe he's lost your number? No! No! No! You're an independent young woman and independent women don't call first! If he's that interested he will call. And just to jog his little memory, cast this spell to ensure he's the one who dials your number.

Ingredients

- A piece of pink paper
- A red pen
- An orange tea-light candle
- Matches or a lighter
- A 6-in. (15-cm) length of pink ribbon
- A phone

Cast this spell on a Friday night. Take the piece of paper and draw a picture of the guy you want to call you. You don't have to be any good at drawing, so long as *you* draw it. Light the orange tea-light candle and say the following once:

I send this wish to the nine Muses
That you will join together and send this
        message to [name]
So that he will not forget me
And will feel compelled to call me
So mote it be.

Fold up the piece of paper and seal it with a little hot wax from the tea-light candle, by carefully tilting it to one side. Allow the wax to cool and then tie the pink ribbon around the paper. Place the paper under your phone and he should call you soon. If you find it difficult to leave the paper under the phone, then put it under your pillow or mattress.

Back off spell

Yes, I agree, parents can be a pain at times, but they really are trying to protect you and not deliberately trying to ruin your life – honest! I'm a parent to three girls and, believe me, parenting doesn't come with a handbook. I've lost count of the amount of times my own parents grounded me, or prevented me from doing something! If you can learn to think that your Mom and Dad were once just like you, and they are only human and trying to help you, you might just see them in a different light. This spell is designed for when you really can't take any more and wish that everyone would just back off for a while. Try it, it does work – just don't tell my Mom I said that!

Ingredients

- A dark blue candle
- A candle holder
- Matches or a lighter
- A bowl
- A teaspoon of salt
- A teaspoon of pepper
- A spoon
- Half a lemon
- Something personal relating to the person bothering you

This spell can apply to anyone who is driving you crazy – so it's not just applicable to parents – and should be done on a waning moon (when the moon is a C-shape). Place the blue candle in a candle holder and light it. Prepare the spell mixture in your bowl as follows.

Put the salt and pepper in the bowl and mix it up. The salt is for protection and the pepper is to banish. Squeeze the juice of half a lemon into the bowl and mix it all up with the spoon. Take the item belonging to the person bothering you and place it underneath or to the left side of the candle. The item could be a photograph, a piece of jewelry, a watch, and so on. Say the following words once:

By the power within me
I command you to stop bothering me now
I must be allowed to make my own choices
Be they wrong or right
I must be allowed to make my own mistakes
and learn by them
May this harmeth none
Now this spell has begun.

Concentrate on the person who has been bothering you for a moment. Dip your index finger into the mixture you have prepared and place a drop behind, to the front, to the left, and to the right of the candle. Then place a tiny amount upon the item belonging to the other person. Allow the candle to burn down safely. Return the item to where you found it and throw the rest of the mixture either in the trash can or in your garden.

You should notice that your Mom or Dad (or the person who has been bothering you) backs off now. This spell is suggestive magick and won't harm anyone, so don't worry.

A happy home life

Do you wish you could have a happy home life just like your friends? Unfortunately for some this isn't possible and they often live in fear of what they will encounter when they go home. This spell is to encourage a happy home life for you. Whether you have problems with your parents, a brother or sister, or someone else within the family who is making your life miserable, try this protection spell to protect you from being hurt, physically or mentally, and create a happy home life for yourself. If you feel that you are in danger or if you are being abused, either physically or mentally, please talk to someone who can help — for example, a teacher, your doctor, the parent of a friend, call a helpline, or seek more professional help.

Ingredients

- A bag of salt
- A bowl
- A teaspoon of cinnamon
- A basil leaf
- An onion
- A knife
- One blue candle
- One white candle
- One green candle
- Three candle holders
- Matches or a lighter
- A 12-in. (30-cm) length of blue ribbon

Do this spell on a waning moon (C-shaped), or on a Thursday. And it's best to perform this spell when there is no one else in the house. If this proves difficult, perform it in your bedroom instead.

Pour half of the salt into the bowl and add the cinnamon and the basil leaf. Cut the onion in half and cover both halves of the onion in the salt and cinnamon mixture. Put the three candles into holders, and light them in this order – blue, green, then white. Say the following words just once:

Athena, warrior Goddess of order and peace
Hear my cry and take hold of this situation
Banish any negativity from my home
So that I feel safe and secure once again
May you protect me always
And release positive energy, healing, and peace
Let no evil come into my home
So mote it be.

While you wait for the candles to burn down, take the mixture with the salt and cinnamon in it and sprinkle every room in the house with it. Go outside and sprinkle as much of the mixture as you can around the outside of your home. Take the two onion halves and tie them together with the blue ribbon. Place the onion and the basil leaf under your bed or hide it somewhere in your room. This powerful spell will banish the fear of going home, protect you from harm, and promote harmony in your home life.

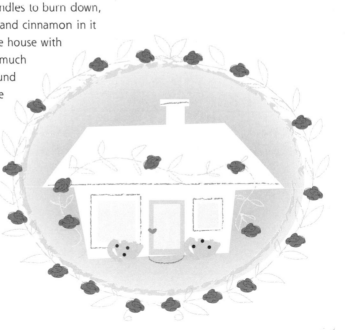

Guy trouble spell

Relationships should be fun but sometimes they're far from it. Whether he's pressuring you into doing something you don't want to do, flirting with everything in a skirt, or just generally behaving badly, this is the spell to give your guy a sharp wake-up call. As with all suggestive magick, this spell will make him think twice about how he's been treating you without your even saying a word to him.

Ingredients

- A hair belonging to him
- A hair belonging to you
- One white tea-light candle
- Matches or a lighter
- A piece of writing paper
- A pen
- A plain envelope
- A heatproof dish

You should do this spell on a Saturday, or when the moon is waning.

As much as he may deserve it, don't go pulling his hair out in order to obtain a hair belonging to him! Much better to secretly take one from a hairbrush. Light the white candle and concentrate on why your guy has annoyed you. Write a letter to him about it all. Don't worry, you can write anything you want, from his annoying habit of flirting with your best friend to pressuring you to sleep with him. Get all your frustrations about him down on paper.

When you've finished, place the letter and the two hairs into the envelope. Hold your right hand over the letter and say the following words:

[name of guy] you will no longer behave badly
To continue will only destroy what we have
I will no longer tolerate this situation
I command you to stop now
This is my wish, so mote it be.

Take the envelope and place it in
the candle flame until it catches
fire. Drop the letter into the
heatproof dish and watch the
flames eat it up, as they do
they will banish the problems
you have with your guy.

Leave me alone spell

Some people just can't take a hint, can they? If you're having problems with a guy who just won't leave you alone, try this banishing balloon spell to get the message across once and for all.

Ingredients

- A piece of paper
- A black pen
- A black balloon

This simple spell is excellent if someone who has set his sights on you just won't take the hint that you're not interested, and is best done on a waning moon or a new (dark) moon.

Write the name of the person in black ink on the piece of paper. Below it write the words LEAVE ME ALONE! Next, rip the paper into tiny pieces and place to one side. Blow up the balloon and hold the top to prevent the air escaping. Carefully push the pieces of paper you ripped up into the balloon. When you've done this tie up the balloon. Take the balloon outside and say the following words:

By the power of the wind
Carry this message to the recipient
Make sure he knows that I am not interested
*   in him*
But that I mean him no harm
Allow me to live my life free of [name]
*   from this moment on*
Thank you, so mote it be.

Close your eyes, hold the balloon up high, and
let go of it. Watch it as it drifts off into the distance.
When you can no longer see the balloon, you can
rest assured this person won't bother you again.

Making friends spell

Some people can make friends just like that, for others it's not so easy. You might be shy or worried about making the first move. You might have had to move away from your hometown, or you've just started a new job and are the new girl in the office. Don't worry, this spell will help you to make and keep new friends.

Ingredients

- *A blank postcard*
- *A gold pen*
- *A bay leaf*
- *Clear adhesive tape*
- *A 12-in. (30-cm) length of thin gold ribbon*

Do this spell on a Sunday or a Wednesday, or on a new (dark) or full moon.

The postcard is to write your request for new friends to enter your life. Take the gold pen and at the top write the word WANTED, then underline it. Now write what kind of friends you would like in your life. You could write something like, *WANTED fun and caring friends at work/school/home who like me for who I am. New friends who I can confide in, go out with, and enjoy myself with.*

When you've done this, stick the bay leaf to the postcard. Carefully roll up the postcard into a tube shape and tie the gold ribbon around it. Leave the scroll on your bedroom windowsill for 24 hours so that your message will be carried to the universe, then place the scroll somewhere in your bedroom. You should soon see new friends entering your life.

A helping hand

Your friends may not be into magick, but that doesn't mean you can't help them with a little practical magick when they're going through a tough time. The only provision when casting a spell for someone else is that you do get their permission. You don't have to say, "Look, I'm a witch and I can cast a spell to make it all better for you." The mere fact that your friend has confided in you is a cry for help. Ask her if she would like you to help. If she asks how you can possibly do anything, simply say you'll do what you can. You will find over time that if and when your friends discover your magickal powers, they will automatically come to you to fix their problems. This is fine, but just make sure that it's a problem that they really need help with and that they're not just being lazy!

Ingredients

- Silver glitter
- Some soft modeling clay
- A bay leaf
- One white tea-light candle
- Matches or a lighter

Cast this spell on any day and any moon phase.

Place some silver glitter in your hands and then roll the soft modeling clay between your hands. As you do this think of your friend's problem. It could be that she's harming herself, has boyfriend troubles, parent problems, school problems. Whatever the problem is, concentrate on the words she used to tell you about her problem.

Next, create a little person out of the glittery modeling clay – this is going to represent your

friend. Put your model on top of the bay leaf. Place
the bay leaf and model behind the white tea-light
candle and light the candle. Say the following words:

Goddess of Athena, please help me to help
   [name]
May you take on this problem
To bring her comfort and healing
So that her problems will fade away
May her worries be gone
And her troubles be banished
May you help in my quest
Thank you, so mote it be.

Allow the candle to burn down
safely. Leave the figure of your friend
on the bay leaf and place this on a
windowsill that catches the morning
sun. Your friend's troubles should soon
diminish. Please bear in mind that this
spell is not a substitute for medical
advice. If you feel that your friend
needs to speak to a professional,
tell her and go along with her.

41

Banish the bully spell

If you find that you're the victim of a bully, whether at school or work, then this spell will work wonders. You cannot hurt anyone with white magick, but this powerful spell will make the person who has been bullying you think twice about doing it again!

Ingredients

- A permanent black marker pen
- A piece of white letter paper
- A matchbox
- A bag of salt
- One black candle
- A candle holder
- Matches or a lighter
- A small mirror
- A 6-in. (15-cm) length of black ribbon

Do this spell on a waning or a new (dark) moon.

First of all take your black marker pen and write on the letter paper in big letters the name of the person who is bullying you. Next, color in the matchbox in black marker pen. Sit on the floor and cast a big circle of salt around you. Place the black candle (in a holder), your piece of paper, the matchbox, the mirror, and the black ribbon in the circle with you. Light the candle and rip the piece of paper up into tiny pieces. When you've done this, put all the pieces of paper in the matchbox. Take a pinch of salt from your circle and put this in the matchbox too. Now tie the matchbox up with the black ribbon. Place the matchbox on top of the mirror and say the following words:

By the power of the universe
You no longer have any control over me
I banish you and send this hurt back to you
You will know how it feels to be bullied
And you will bully no more
So mote it be.

Blow out the candle and step out of your circle. Take the matchbox as far away as you can from your home. This spell is designed to not only protect you but to stop this person from bullying you ever again, and it is amazingly powerful. Unfortunately few workplaces have a bullying policy, but don't let that discourage you. Make sure you talk to someone who you can trust in personnel. Nowadays most schools have a no-bullying policy, so use it. By speaking up and confronting the bully, in work or at school, hopefully bullying will become a thing of the past.

Get that job spell

Have you spent your allowance before you've even gotten it? Are you being nagged to death to get a job? Or are you fed up with being broke all the time and just need a regular injection of cash? This spell will help you to land a job to suit your needs — whether it's to pay for your everyday living expenses or to buy that designer dress you've got your eye on. Try it, it works!

Ingredients

- *A piece of green letter paper*
- *A gold pen*
- *Three mint leaves*
- *A teaspoon of dried sage*
- *A teaspoon of silver glitter*
- *One gold or silver candle*
- *A candle holder*
- *Matches or a lighter*

You should cast this spell on a full moon, waxing moon, or on a Thursday.

Draw a large pentagram in the center of your piece of paper with your gold pen – a pentagram is a circle with a five-pointed star inside it. Make sure the star points upward not downward. In the center of the pentagram write the word JOB. Around this word write what kind of job you want – part-time, full-time, in an office, how many hours, how much you'd like to be paid, and so on. Tear up the mint leaves and put these, the dried sage, and the silver glitter into the pentagram. Place the candle in a holder on top of the herbs and light it. Say the following words:

Goddess Morrigan, hear my plea
Send me a job to help my needs
Give me a job that I will love
I send this message to you above.

Allow the candle to burn down. Carefully take the paper with the herbs and glitter on it to the nearest window, open the window, and blow the contents from the paper into the air. You will soon hear about a job that will interest you or you might see an advertisement for the ideal job for you.

Witchy info

Christians once used the pentagram as a religious symbol. Each point represented the five wounds of Christ. To pagans and witches it represents Morrigan, the war goddess who fights for peace and good fortune for others. If you see the pentagram drawn with the top point of the star pointing to the bottom of the circle, this represents dark and sinister magick, so always draw your pentagram with the top point of the star pointing upward.

Interview success spell

We all get nervous at the prospect of an interview, but with a little practical magick you will breeze through it and impress that interviewer to boot.

Ingredients

- A small blue envelope
- One pale blue candle
- A candle holder
- A teaspoon of dried peppermint
- A teaspoon of gold glitter
- Matches or a lighter
- A piece of paper
- An item of blue clothing

Cast this spell the night before your interview.

Place the blue envelope in front of the candle and place the peppermint and the gold glitter on top of the envelope. Mix the herbs and glitter together with your index finger and light the candle in its holder. Say the following words six times:

Magick Mix, Magick Blue
Help me with this interview
I give power to this spell
Please do the rest
Let them see that I'm the best.

While the candle is burning down, shake the herbs onto a clean piece of paper and then pour them into the blue envelope. Seal the envelope with a little hot wax from the candle and place the envelope in your purse or pocket to take with you to the interview.

When you go to the interview wear a hidden item of blue clothing – this could be a handkerchief or blue underwear for example. Just before the interview, shake your blue envelope for extra luck.

Remember, if you don't get the job, it doesn't mean the spell hasn't worked. It just means this particular job isn't for you and a more suitable one will be along soon.

Protecting your car spell

Your first car is one of the most important things in a girl's life — it gives you your independence, after all. Obviously you must have your car insured, but this spell will give it that extra magickal insurance and protect your prized possession.

Ingredients

- Four drops of lavender oil
- Four drops of bergamot oil
- Four drops of rose oil
- Four drops of peppermint oil
- A small bowl
- A model of your car
- Paper towel

Cast this spell on a Thursday or a full moon.

The model of your car doesn't need to be precisely like the car you drive; see if you can find one of a similar color if you can't find the exact model. Mix all the oils together in a small bowl and say the following words once:

Almighty God of Protection
I ask that you protect my car
From fire, theft, or third party damage
May I always be safe when traveling.

Place the model car in the oil and wipe the oil all over it, then take it out and dab it dry with a paper towel. Place the model car in the glove compartment of your real car. This will protect your car and keep you safe when traveling.

Please do not use this spell as an alternative to auto insurance!

Protection spell for your new apartment

Although it might be new to you, your apartment might still have negative vibes floating around from a previous occupant. This cleansing and protection spell will cleanse any negativity from your apartment and protect it from intruders, fire, floods, or any other unwanted guests!

Ingredients

- 3½ oz (100 g) of salt
- 16 fl oz (500 ml) of bottled water
- A jug
- A whole onion
- A knife
- One seashell for every room in your apartment/house

Cast this spell on a new (dark) moon or a Saturday.

Pour the salt into the water and shake gently. Next, pour the salted water into a jug. Now cut the onion into four quarters. Sprinkle a few drops of salted water onto each quarter of onion and place one quarter in each corner of the main room you use in your apartment. Sprinkle each seashell with the salt mixture and place a seashell in every room in your apartment. Finally, walk into each room and sprinkle a few drops of the salted water into each room. Say the following words as you enter each room:

This room is now protected and cleansed.

Leave the onion in the main room for one week as this will absorb any negativity in the home. Leave

the seashells where they are and every so often
re-cleanse them with a new protection salt mixture.
Your apartment will now be magickally insured
and protected.

Financing your life

The Goddess is not adverse to a little practical magick to help you get what you want in life — she is a girlie girl after all and thinks that every woman deserves a treat from time to time! So long as you don't expect to cast a spell and never have to work again, you can use this spell for all your needs and desires, be it new DVDs, new clothes, music, a computer, even that nice handbag you've seen!

Ingredients

- An image representing your desire
- Scissors
- Some glue
- A piece of white letter paper
- A pen
- An envelope
- A silver coin
- One silver candle
- A candle holder
- Matches or a lighter

Cast this spell on a Wednesday or a waxing moon.

The image of your desire could be a clipping from a magazine, such as a pair of shoes you've had your eye on. Cut the picture out and stick it onto the white paper. Write next to it why you want this item — what pleasure will you get from it?

Fold the paper up and place it in the envelope along with the silver coin. Light the silver candle in its holder and say the following words:

Oh Money Lord hear my plea
Send this item on to me
May I have the funds that I require
To buy this item and make me smile.

Allow the candle to burn down and sleep with
the envelope under your pillow for seven nights. You
should soon see an improvement in your finances so
that you are able to buy the item you want.
Alternatively, you might be given it as a gift.

A spell to find a new apartment

You might be thinking about moving out of your parents' home for the first time, looking for an apartment near college to rent, or even looking for a bigger and better apartment than the one you're living in now. Either way, try this spell to find the ideal apartment for you.

Ingredients

- One orange candle
- A candle holder
- A small gold-colored curtain ring
- A newspaper with a housing section in it
- Matches or a lighter
- Scissors

Cast this spell on a new (dark) moon.

Place the orange candle in a holder, and put it and the curtain ring on top of the newspaper opened at the housing section. Light the candle and say the following words:

I send this message to the universe
So that you may help in finding the right home
*   for me*
May it be peaceful, safe, and a happy place
This is my wish, so mote it be.

When the candle has burned down, cut a house shape out of the newspaper. Roll your house shape up into a tube shape and place the golden curtain ring over it. Keep this charm with you until you find the right property, which should be soon.

Banish zits lotion

Yes, we all get zits — even models — and at the most inconvenient times too, such as when you're going on a date for the first time. If your face suddenly breaks out in lumps and bumps, try this natural magickal lotion to zap the zits for good. Please note: If you suffer from bad acne, this lotion is not a substitute for medical advice.

Ingredients

- 3 oz (85 g) of marigold flowers
- 2 fl oz (50 ml) of distilled (pure) water
- A wide-mouthed jar with a lid
- A bottle with a lid
- A tea strainer

You should pepare this lotion whenever you need to zap some zits.

You can buy Calendula, a ready-made homeopathic remedy for zits, that you simply apply as instructed. If you can't find this remedy, you can easily make your own, as instructed below.

Dry the marigold flowers on a warm windowsill until they become crisp, then chop them up finely. Add the chopped flowers to the distilled water and pour this into the jar. Allow to stew for a few hours. Shake the jar to mix the lotion up. After a few hours, strain the lotion into a bottle using the tea strainer.

Apply this lotion three times daily by using a cotton ball. You can keep this lotion for up to two weeks.

Bad hair days' shampoo

Yep, it's another thing we girls have to put up with — bad hair days and you can guarantee you'll have one the very day you want to look your best. Never fear, magick is here in the form of a luscious shampoo that will guarantee glossy hair and banish bad hair days forever.

Ingredients

- 4 oz (115 g) of dried soapwort
- 1 pint (600 ml) of boiling water
- Two jugs
- A tea strainer
- Half a lemon
- An egg

This is one of the most fantastic natural shampoos that will make your hair glossy, shiny, and lovely. Make it whenever you have a BHD.

The herb soapwort is available from an herbalist or a pharmacy. Pop the soapwort into the boiling water in a jug and leave to steep for ten minutes. Strain the mixture into the second jug and allow to cool. Add the juice of half a lemon and gently beat in the egg. You can now wash your hair with the shampoo as you would use a normal shampoo. If you wish to keep some of the shampoo, leave the egg out of the recipe and store the lotion in an old plastic shampoo bottle.

Once you've experienced the results you'll never want to buy a cosmetic shampoo again!

59

To cast a beauty aura before a big date

We all want to look our best for that big date. This spell will make you look and feel wonderful inside and out.

Ingredients

- Your favorite bubble bath
- A big fluffy towel
- A full-length mirror
- Four pink candles
- Four candle holders
- Your favorite lipstick
- Your favorite perfume
- Matches or a lighter

Cast this spell just prior to going out for the night.

First of all, run yourself a big bubbly bath and relax in it for at least 15 minutes. Wrap a towel around you and sit in front of your mirror. Place your four pink candles in candle holders in a line in front of the mirror. Put your favorite lipstick on and your perfume and finally light the candles.

Look at yourself in the mirror and imagine an aura of beauty and confidence filling up inside you from the tips of your toes to the top of your head. Take this process slowly and feel how warm you feel as the aura expands up and up through your body. Try to maintain this state for ten minutes. When you feel happy, blow out the candles and get yourself dressed. You will not only feel fantastic, but you will look fantastic for your date.

Where dreams come true

Did you know you have the power to make every dream you have come true with a little help from the power of magick? Well, you do have that power. For everything from passing your exams to gaining entry into university, to making lifelong friends and having a fantastic social life, magick can make all your dreams come true, if you really believe it can. However, magick will only work if you know what it is you do and don't want in your life. It doesn't work if you have no idea of what your dreams are, or where you are heading.

This chapter is dedicated to deciding what you want out of life and is the basis of showing you how to decide this by making your very own Funky Dream Board! I devised the Dream Board while working on a project about mind magick and have adapted it to suit you. This is a great way of deciding what your dreams are and how you are going to accomplish them.

We all have things we want in life, be it the latest computer or being able to afford a deposit on your own apartment. This is the place where you can be truly imaginative and create whatever it is you want in your life. This is the place where anything and everything is possible, so go wild!

The Funky Dream Board runs in conjunction with the spells in this book, so as soon as you decide what it is you want in your life, create your Dream Board and, for that extra bit of magick, cast one of the spells in this book that applies to your dreams.

Funky Dream Board

This is a great thing to do on your own, or gather a few friends together and make a really girlie night of it. Either way, make your FDB on a new (dark) or a full moon.

Ingredients

- *A large piece of cardboard in your favorite color*
- *Some colored pens*
- *Some sticky stars*
- *Some glitter in different colors*
- *Some dried flowers/potpourri*
- *Some glue*
- *A selection of magazines*
- *Scissors*

First of all place the piece of cardboard on the floor in front of you and think of it as a clean sheet. From now on, this is going to be the new you. Forget about any problems from the past. The past is the past. Forget about the trouble you had getting through your last exam, or the arguments with your parents, or getting into debt, and so on. This is a brand new start for you.

Next, write in big letters *My Funky Dream Board – Where Wishes Come True* across the top of the cardboard. You can decorate this title with stars, glitter, dried flowers, feathers, and so on to make it look better.

The most important thing with your FDB is to make sure the things you put on there are the things *you* want, not your parents' wishes, not your friends' wishes, *your* wishes. You'll find it easier to start off with small things, so think about something small that you want right now. A new cell phone perhaps? OK, now look through the magazines and find the phone that you want. Cut it out and stick it on your FDB. Next to the picture write something like, "I can

now afford to buy this new cell phone." Don't even
think about the fact that you might have
only a few cents in your purse right now.
This simple, positive statement is
enough to make your dream of owning
that new cell phone soon become a reality.

Now go on to something else you want in your
life, say in a few months' time. It could be to have a
better social life, or to have an extension on your
curfew. It could be that you want
a nice young man in your life, or you
want to pass your driving test.
Whatever it is you want to achieve,
cut out an image that represents
your wish and stick it onto
your Dream Board. You
might have fallen into
a bad habit such as smoking
and want to give it up. If
this is the case stick an
image of a full ashtray with a
red cross through it onto your
Dream Board or a pile of
money representing the
amount of spare cash
you'll have when you do
give it up.

The purpose of the
Funky Dream Board is that
you build up a series of your
ideal life in picture form. Every time you

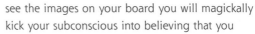

see the images on your board you will magickally kick your subconscious into believing that you deserve these things and, more importantly, you will have these things in your life. By looking at your FDB on a daily basis and believing that you can attain these dreams you will make them come true. The subconscious can't distinguish between what is a true or a false statement, so the more you tell your subconscious that you have these things, the more your subconscious believes and your whole attitude will change. As a result you will attract new opportunities – the right opportunities, so that you will in turn attract more money to buy the material things on your Dream Board and everything else you want in life.

Additional magick comes in when you apply the glitter to your Funky Dream Board. When you feel you have finished all the pictures and captions on your Dream Board, dot lots of glue around the pictures, hold the glitter in your hands and whisper,

Dream Board, Dream Board, I command you, make all my wishes and dreams come true.

Now blow the glitter all over your Dream Board. Shake any excess glitter off and your dream board is now magickally enchanted.

How a Dream Board can work

Let me give you an example of how a Dream Board can work. Say, for example, you presently look like any other average girl and your shyness is preventing you from doing what you want, but deep down you long for a great social life, a handsome boyfriend, and to become a model for a top New York agency. You would stick an image of how you would like to look onto your Dream Board, with a caption such as, "I am a beautiful looking young woman who has a fantastic social life full of loving friends. I have a wonderful boyfriend who treats me like a princess and I've been signed with a top model agency and my life is great!"

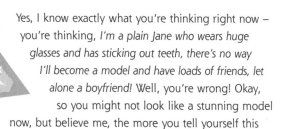

Yes, I know exactly what you're thinking right now – you're thinking, *I'm a plain Jane who wears huge glasses and has sticking out teeth, there's no way I'll become a model and have loads of friends, let alone a boyfriend!* Well, you're wrong! Okay, so you might not look like a stunning model now, but believe me, the more you tell yourself this is what you will become, the more you will change. Not overnight, but you will become exactly what you want to be and attract the kind of life you want.

As soon as you change the way you feel about yourself, you will change the way you look and behave. As with the above example, you might suddenly decide that instead of having short hair you will get extensions and arrange with a dentist to straighten your teeth. Next time you have to go to the opticians you might decide to try contact lenses instead of glasses. In just three simple steps you've already changed your appearance. You'll look in the mirror and suddenly realize that you *are* beautiful and all it took was a little makeover. The more you change, the more confidence you'll have and this will show at school or at work. You will suddenly notice that people look at you differently because you are more confident and the invitations will start flooding in! See – all it takes is a little belief.

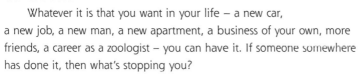

Whatever it is that you want in your life – a new car, a new job, a new man, a new apartment, a business of your own, more friends, a career as a zoologist – you can have it. If someone somewhere has done it, then what's stopping you?

Believe and you will get what you want in every area of your life.

What if I don't know what I want?

Some people have said to me, "What if I don't know what I want?" Well here's a simple way to discover what it is you want in your life – look at what it is you don't want. If you already have everything you want in your life then you're a very lucky girl. But for those who are not sure, this easy test will show you what it is that you would like in your life.

Take a separate piece of paper and write down all the things you don't want. This could be something like, you're fed up with fighting with your parents all the time, or you don't want to go to school or work because you hate it. You could hate the fact that you decided to study medicine because all your friends were doing it, or you might not be so keen on the idea of moving in with your boyfriend. Whatever you don't feel 100 percent comfortable with, write it down on your list.

Now you can look through the list and change it into what you do want. So from the list above we would change it to something like, *I get along very well with my parents now and they are very proud of me, we never argue now. I have excelled at school, or I now have a job that I love. I have changed my degree to study something I truly love doing. I have bought my own apartment and I live on my own and I am happy with this.* So for everything that you hate in your life right now, you can soon fix it by applying the opposite to what you don't want to something you'd rather have.

You will soon know what it is that you do want out of life – and the sure sign is when you get that buzz of excitement when you think about achieving your dreams. This sign means that this is what you really want.

It's important to balance the things you want in your life, too. For example, when I had my first daughter I was still working full time. I longed to have more time to spend with my daughter and this is one of the things I put on my Dream Board. Within three months the company I worked for closed and all the employees, including me, were laid off. Whoops! I had plenty of time to spend with my daughter, but I had no money to pay the bills!

If, say, your love life was loveless and you decided you wanted lots of attention from the opposite sex, what are you going to do if you attract all these new wonderful men into your life and they *all* want to take you out on Saturday night? So be specific, and think ahead as to what complications could arise.

A Book of Shadows

Every budding girlie witch should have her own Book of Shadows! A Book of Shadows is like a witches' diary where you put all your witchy information. This might be spells that you come across or make yourself, different phases of the moon, and anything that you need to remember about spell casting.

Your Book of Shadows should last you a long time, so it's worth investing in something that is going to last. A hard-backed book with plain pages is ideal and you can decorate it as outrageously as you like. Keep your Book of Shadows safe. It will come in handy when you need to refer to a particular spell again.

Techno witch

When the religion of Wicca first came about, believers would call upon the power of nature to help them gain what they wanted in life because this is all they had to use. Over the years I've studied many records of the use of witchcraft, and although the basic principles of witchcraft and spell casting remain the same, many of the spells witches would use in the old days simply couldn't be applied to today's modern world.

For example, one spell I came across was to find your perfect partner. The ingredients included a barrel full of oak leaves, a barrel full of stinging nettles and you were instructed to roll sky-clad (naked) in the morning dew. Can you imagine performing this spell in today's world? Okay, so even if you managed to get away with stripping an entire forest of its life force, and refrain from getting stung by a field of stinging nettles, imagine what your neighbors would think of seeing you rolling around on the lawn at six o'clock in the morning!

As with everything, we have to adapt to the modern world and that includes practical magick. Many followers of The Craft believe that we should hold onto the ancient traditions that have been handed down over the years, and I agree, up to a certain point. But we also have to move with the times. Just as with the intervention of medicine we no longer die from a cold, we can easily adapt our magickal skills to fit in with the modern world we live in.

This chapter deals with using practical magick in the modern world, including spells to protect your computer from viruses and from crashing, connection spells for your cell phone, and how your computer can come in handy when you want that extra little bit of techno magick in your life.

The speed at which we can connect to people on the other side of the world is amazingly quick and it has to travel the entire universe, what better way to get your prayers answered?

Banish computer crashes

Gone are the days when our only means of communication was the postal system — thank goodness! The modern girl now uses a computer to communicate to the world. And boy, what a pain in the butt it can be when it crashes! This spell is designed to protect your computer from crashing at the most inappropriate times! Do this spell on a Monday evening.

Ingredients

- A small rose quartz
- 2 teaspoons of salt
- 2 fl oz (50 ml) of water
- A 12-in. (30-cm) length of pink ribbon
- One long pink candle
- A candle holder
- Matches or a lighter

Rose quartz is a natural pink crystal that is available in all crystal/New Age shops and comes in all shapes and sizes. When you are choosing your rose quartz, pick one that you feel drawn to. It doesn't have to be big, just choose the one you most like. Crystals absorb negative energy and the rose quartz is the prettiest crystal I know of — ideal for the witchy girl!

Make the salt water by mixing two teaspoons of salt to 2 fl oz (50 ml) of tap water and place the rose quartz in the salt water. Salt is a natural protection source. Leave the quartz in the salt solution for half an hour.

Allow the quartz to dry naturally on a sunny windowsill. When it is dry, wrap the pink ribbon around the rose quartz and place it on top of your computer monitor/screen.

Place the pink candle in a candle holder nearby, light it, and say the following words once:

By the power of the universe
By the power in me
Protect the workings in my PC
Ensure no crashes
Ensure no faults
Protect my PC
With this quartz and salt.

Allow the candle to burn down safely. Leave the rose quartz to sit on your computer. Refresh the spell by repeating it once a week.

When you repeat the spell, use the same crystal and pink ribbon, but make a new solution of salt water and use a new pink candle.

Success story

I designed this spell when my PC had been hit by a nasty virus that destroyed all my documents. I managed to retrieve them, eventually, but vowed that this would not happen again. And thankfully it hasn't. I passed this spell on to all my girlfriends, who all swear by it.

Cosmic connections

It's always the way, isn't it? The very moment you need to make that important call you can't get a signal on your cell phone. Never fear, this spell will ensure that you get connected. It will also give your cell phone extra magickal life, so that it doesn't let you down at that crucial moment.

Ingredients

- A piece of green material 12 in. x 12 in. (30 cm x 30 cm)
- Some glue
- Some silver glitter
- Some green glitter
- Some green thread
- A needle
- Your phone charger
- Your cell phone (switched off)
- A 12-in. (30-cm) length of green ribbon

See – you knew there was a reason why you took Home Ec. at school! This little skill will come in handy because you need to make a magickal pouch for your cell phone. First of all, drop several dots of glue on what will be the outer side of the green material and, before it dries, sprinkle the silver and green glitter all over it. When this is dry shake off any excess glitter and fold the material in half, so that it forms a long pocket. Sew up the bottom and one long side with the green thread.

Do this spell once a week on any day. Make sure you switch on your battery charger and plug it into your phone, but keep the phone switched off. Place the phone in your magickal pouch and tie the green ribbon around it. Close your eyes and say the following words:

Advice using this spell

It may sound obvious but often all it takes is to move around a bit and your connection will appear. The Goddess will help you once you've performed this spell, but don't overlook the obvious. If you leave your phone uncharged, the battery will run down and no amount of magick will make it work! Also, remember to repeat this spell once a week. You should soon notice that your cell phone has optimum performance and lasts much longer.

By the power of the universe
May you protect this means of communication
So that it is always there
For whenever I need it
So mote it be.

Leave the phone to charge up, then take the phone out of the pouch. You should now never have any problems getting a connection when you are out and about.

Cell phone magick

We can now get our message across to another person — who might be on the other side of the world — in the split second it takes to press the send button and this is one of the most powerful ways to communicate your wishes to the universe. This great techno-witch wishing spell is an ideal way to send your wishes to be granted by the universe.

Ingredients

• Your cell phone

Cast this spell on the following days:

Sunday – for success
Monday – for health
Tuesday – for protection
Wednesday – for exams/tests
Thursday – for good luck
Friday – for love/friendship
Saturday – for banishing something

Decide what you want your wish for and do the spell on that day; so, for example, if you've fallen out with your friend and want to make up, do the spell on a Friday. If you wanted extra luck for an exam or a driving test, you would do the spell on a Wednesday. Concentrate on your wish for a moment and then type in the following words in a text message:

Your wish is my command

Now send the text message to your *own* cell phone number. Moments later you will receive a text message. Read the words from the text message and believe that your wish has now been carried right around the universe and is being granted as we speak. The more times you send this message to yourself, the more power you give to your wish being granted.

Digital magick

*This is a great techno spell to do if you own a digital camera
and it will make you feel wonderful!*

Ingredients

- Your favorite clothes
- A digital camera
- A PC
- An imaging program

This spell is great if you're feeling a bit low about yourself and need to boost your self-esteem. Cast this spell on a new (dark) moon.

After a lovely warm bath, dress in your favorite outfit, dry your hair, and make yourself look stunning. Don't worry about the zit on your nose or the baggy eyes from being out too late, we can fix that in a minute.

Either set your digital camera on auto or get a friend or relative to take a couple of photos of you. Now for the fun bit!

Choose the best photo of yourself and put it into your imaging program on your computer. Now experiment with brush art taking out all the bits you don't like about yourself, such as the zit on your nose, the red eyes, or even your hair color. You can have great fun playing around with making yourself look fantastic — after all, all the celebrities on the covers of magazines are air brushed!

Add personal dream images to your photo. So, for example, if your dream is to be a teacher, place the image of a blackboard in the background of your picture. If you dream of rock climbing, put an image of some mountains behind you. Create how you would like to be. There are no restrictions when you dream and when you do dream for long enough, you create reality. When you've finished either print your picture out and pop it in a picture frame or save it as your wallpaper on your computer.

Every time you're feeling down, look at this picture and tell yourself how utterly fantastic you really are!

Wishing pyramid

This spell is a modern version of a wishing spell that has been used with great success for many years. The shape of the pyramid is believed by cultures all over the world to have magickal powers and was especially believed by the Egyptians to hold mystical and unexplained powers.

Ingredients

- A computer
- A writing program such as Microsoft Word

Cast this spell on any day of the week.

Create a new document in your writing program and name it "My Wish." Click on the document you have created and think of the wish you would like to be granted. Now set the document up so that your cursor is in the center of the page and type the same way as I have illustrated below. For this example I am creating a wish for success to pass an exam.

I
I wish
I wish to
I wish to pass
I wish to pass my
I wish to pass my chemistry
I wish to pass my chemistry exam

As you can see, from the words I've used to grant my wish, I've created a magickal pyramid. Now click the save button to save your wish. The next time you use your computer, take a moment to go into your document named as "My Wish." Underneath the first pyramid leave two clear lines of space and create a second pyramid. Continue to do this once every day until you end up with several pyramids. The more times you create this repeated wish the more powerful it will become. Keep doing this until your wish is granted and then you can wipe this document from your files.

Fortune-telling

Wouldn't it be great to know what was going to happen to you, or the answer to a question, in the future? Well, you can easily read your own future and that of your friends by reading this chapter – which is dedicated to fortune-telling.

In this chapter I will explain a few different forms of divination that you can use to discover what the future has in store for you. Whether you choose to read tarot cards, a crystal ball, or tea leaves, don't assume that the outcome is ever set in stone – it's not. All forms of divination should be thought of as a guide to the possible outcome if you continue on the road that you are taking. So, for example, if you were wondering if you should date a particular boy who your parents and friends disapproved of (with good reason) and you did a tarot reading for your future regarding this boy, you might be told from the cards that it will only end in misery if you choose to follow this particular path. It doesn't mean that your entire future is doomed!

The most important thing to remember when you do any divination is to trust your intuition – a witches' intuition is always right! If you don't fully understand what the tools you are using for divination mean, trust what you feel inside. The tools will guide you, but they can't make a decision for you, only you can do that.

There are many different tools you can use for fortune-telling and in this section I will tell you about a few of them that work well when foreseeing the future.

Terrific tarot cards

You can buy a set of tarot cards from almost any bookstore now and they all come with instructions on how to use them. Whereas years ago there were only a handful of designs available, now you can get tarot cards in all sorts of fun patterns. Regardless of the design all have exactly the same format — 78 cards, which are divided into two parts: the Major Arcana, consisting of 22 cards, and the Minor Arcana, consisting of four suits of 14 cards in each suit.

Success story

I first learned how to read tarot cards when I was 13 years old and have used them ever since with great success. I find that quite often the cards will give me a warning when I feel absolutely sure that I'm doing the right thing, only to find out weeks later they were right. It doesn't matter how rebellious or determined you feel about a decision, if it's not for you the cards will forewarn you.

Whenever you buy a set of tarot cards, choose one that appeals to you and familiarize yourself with it before you do any readings. Shuffle the pack in your hands until the cards become slightly worn — new cards can easily stick to one another. If you can, try to buy or make a small pouch to keep them in when you're not using them. If you take care of your cards, they will take care of you.

There are many different readings you can do with tarot cards, but due to limited space I will tell you how to do a simple question and answer spread. If you wish to know more you can get some excellent books on tarot reading.

Shuffle the cards while you think of a question you want answered. When you feel ready, pick out six cards from anywhere in the pack and lay them face down on the table in front of you. Finally, pick out one more card – this will be your outcome card.

Starting from the left to right, turn over each card and read the meaning from the reference book or table that is included in your pack. The last card is considered as your outcome card, meaning that this will be the outcome of your question. It is important that you interpret the cards to your question. So for example, if you were asking a question about whether you would get a job and the hangman card showed up, it doesn't mean that you are going to be hung! The hangman means waiting around for a while longer, just as the death card doesn't mean that you are gong to die, it means that you are going to be burying the past and can look forward to a bright new future.

Funky prediction pendulum

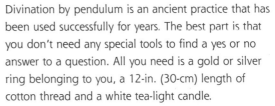

So many questions and not enough answers for the modern girl to find! That can be the problem with life, can't it? Should you go out with Simon or David? Will you pass your math exam? Will your birthday party go as planned? All these questions, it makes you feel dizzy just thinking about it, doesn't it? Never fear, help is at hand with this simple divination by pendulum, or as I like to call it, "the funky prediction pendulum."

Ingredients

- A white tea-light candle
- A 12-in. (30-cm) length of pink cotton thread
- A gold or silver ring belonging to you

Divination by pendulum is an ancient practice that has been used successfully for years. The best part is that you don't need any special tools to find a yes or no answer to a question. All you need is a gold or silver ring belonging to you, a 12-in. (30-cm) length of cotton thread and a white tea-light candle.

You can do this whenever you have a yes or no question you want answered. You do need peace and quiet when doing this form of divination, so tell the family you're doing very important homework and must not be disturbed. Then shut your bedroom door.

Light the tea-light candle and then thread the cotton through your ring. Tie the two ends together and your thread will now be 6-in. (15-cm) long with your ring hanging from the bottom of it.

To find out how the pendulum will answer yes and no, ask it a simple question such as, "is the sun hot?"

After a few seconds the pendulum will either swing from left to right or swing in a circle. This is your yes signal. Ask the pendulum a question you know will produce a no answer, such as "is a ball square?" You should notice that the pendulum swings a different way to your "yes" question.

Now you are ready to ask your own question. Concentrate on your question in your mind, close your eyes and keep asking the question in your head. Open your eyes and you will notice the ring will swing for either yes or no. If the pendulum doesn't move, hold the ring in your hand for a moment and ask again. If you still have no luck then it means that it is not the time to ask that question, so try another.

Success story

Divination by pendulum is one of the oldest divination tools. You do have to make sure that you ask a yes or no question, so if you're wondering which guy to go out with, you would ask, "should I go out with David?" With a little practice you will soon have the answers to all your questions.

Telling tea leaves

It is believed that tea-leaf readings were first introduced by the Romany gypsies as an accurate way of telling the fortune of the avid tea drinker. Before the introduction of tea bags, tea was served loose and brewed in a teapot.

Today you can still read tea leaves, and it's still relatively simple to carry out. You will need a small teapot, a wide-mouthed cup (not a mug) and saucer, a tea bag, some boiled water, and of course, you must like the taste of tea!

Boil a kettle of water and rip open the tea bag and empty the leaves into the teapot. Pour the boiled water into the teapot and wait for a minute for it to brew. While you are waiting, think about what you want the reading to answer. Pour yourself a cup of tea. It's best not to add milk to the tea as this will leave a residue in the cup making your reading harder to see. You now need to drink the tea. It might seem strange at first seeing all these tea leaves floating around in your cup, but you won't get a reading if you don't use tea leaves.

Drink enough of the tea so that there is about one teaspoon of liquid left in the cup. Hold the cup in your left hand and move it in an

counterclockwise circle three times. Now turn the cup upside down on top of the saucer and wait for a minute to enable the remaining liquid to drain away.

Tip the cup upright with your right hand. On first glance you may think that the remaining tea leaves look like nothing in particular. Carefully turn the cup around so that you can look at the leaves from a different angle. You will soon see a series of pictures or symbols in the bottom of your cup. Because of limited space, I have included only a few symbols or pictures you might see in your cup.

Signs that good things are about to happen are: A horseshoe. An acorn. A bridge. A bull. An angel. A basket of flowers. A bee. Birds. A dove. An elephant. A fish. An anchor. A crown. A daffodil. A swan. A ship. A rose.

Signs that something not so good is going to happen are: A bat. Clouds. A coffin. An owl. A rat. A raven. A dagger. A flag. A gun. A sword. A snake. A cross. A monkey. A drum. A mouse.

There are some great books on the market that give you an A–Z of what you might find in the bottom of your cup of tea. If you are thinking about doing tea-leaf readings, you will stand a much better chance of a successful reading if you limit the amount of readings you do. It's best not to do more than two readings in any one week, otherwise your readings will become unclear and confused.

Success story

I've only tried tea-leaf reading a couple of times, because I don't generally drink tea! But on the few times I've done a reading I've found it quite successful. It's a bit hard at first to decipher what the shapes are in the bottom of the cup, but if you keep turning the cup and really look you will soon see shapes or symbols emerging. The last reading I did using tea leaves produced the shape of a baby. A few months later I discovered that I was expecting my second daughter!

Crystal gazing

Divination by crystal gazing has been practiced for years and is coming back into fashion as one of the most successful forms of fortune-telling. Otherwise known as scrying, crystal gazing acts as a medium for clairvoyance. It is widely believed that everybody has the psychic ability to tap into the unknown, but the majority of us don't use this natural skill with which we are all born. The times when you answer the phone and you know instantly who it is on the other end are examples of clairvoyancy. As soon as you realize that you actually have this amazing power, you can put it to good use by knowing exactly what's around the corner.

Success story

A friend of mine swears by crystal gazing and uses a crystal ball for doing readings. She has predicted everything from births, deaths, world disasters, and politics. To date, she's never been wrong!

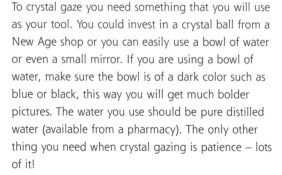

To crystal gaze you need something that you will use as your tool. You could invest in a crystal ball from a New Age shop or you can easily use a bowl of water or even a small mirror. If you are using a bowl of water, make sure the bowl is of a dark color such as blue or black, this way you will get much bolder pictures. The water you use should be pure distilled water (available from a pharmacy). The only other thing you need when crystal gazing is patience – lots of it!

Try to find a time when you have the house to yourself and you can empty your thoughts of everyday things. You should be comfortable and warm and it's best to keep the room you're working in as dark as possible. You should never try to crystal gaze directly after a meal. Close your eyes for a few minutes. Think for a moment about what question you want to be answered. Now begin to look into your chosen tool for divination. Try to be patient. You will not suddenly see an image at first, but the longer you look, you will soon see an image forming. I suggest for your first try you should sit for only ten minutes. If you try to do it for any longer you will give yourself a headache. If you don't see anything the first time, don't worry. Try again the following day and the day after that and soon you will see something emerge from your crystal gazing.

Sometimes you might see colors emerge from your crystal ball, mirror, or water bowl. Light colors are always a good sign, while darker ones are warnings. Images of clouds coming towards you indicate a "yes" answer to a question. Images of clouds going away from you indicate the answer "no." Often you will see the face of a person you know, so pay attention to your intuition as to what you are being told about this person.

As with any form of divination, don't overdo it. If it doesn't work the first time, rest and try again. If you still have no luck, leave it for a week and go back to it. If you are crystal gazing by bowl and water, make sure you refresh the water every time you use it.

Index

Acknowledgments

Executive Editor Brenda Rosen
Managing Editor Clare Churly
Executive Art Editor Sally Bond
Designer Pia Hietarinta for Cobalt id
Illustrator Annie Boberg
Production Controller Aileen O'Reilly